Color Me Elibeth Warren

by Leslie Tran

Color Me Elizabeth Warren

Copyright © 2017 by Leslie Tran

Cover and Illustrations by: Leslie Tran

ISBN-13: 978-0-9978476-6-6
ISBN-10: 0-9978476-6-2

Give feedback on the book at:
Mr.LeslieTran@gmail.com

Printed in U.S.A

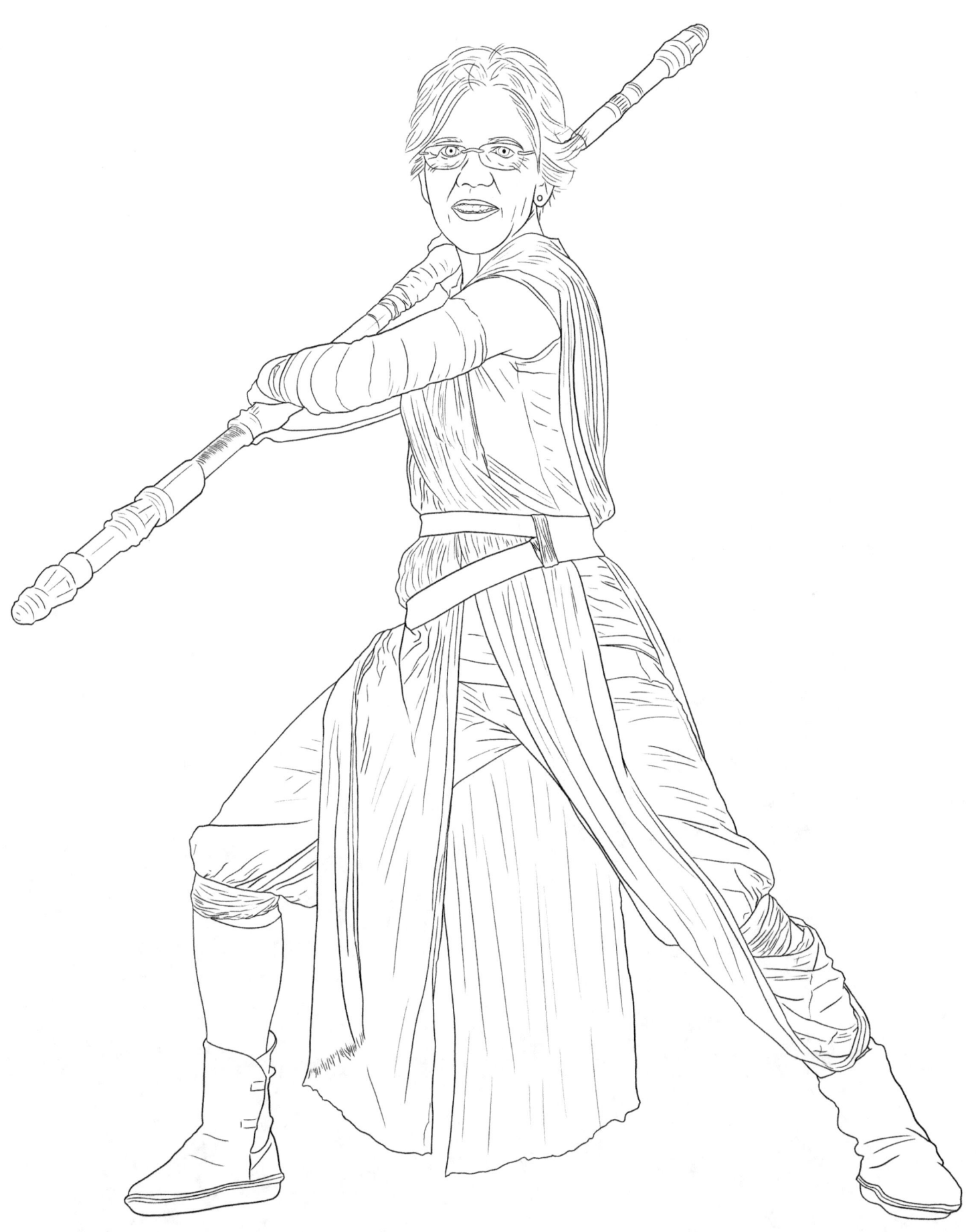

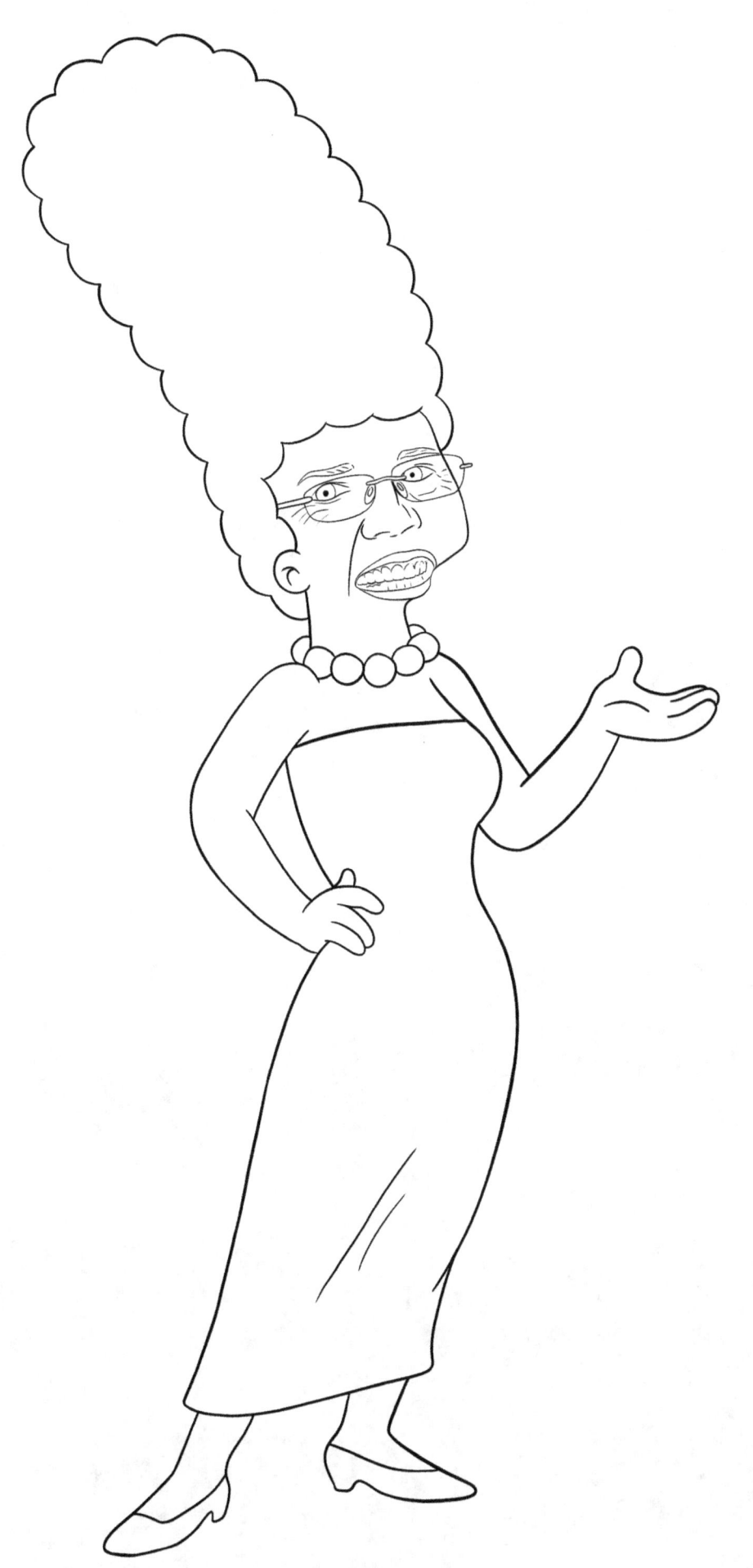

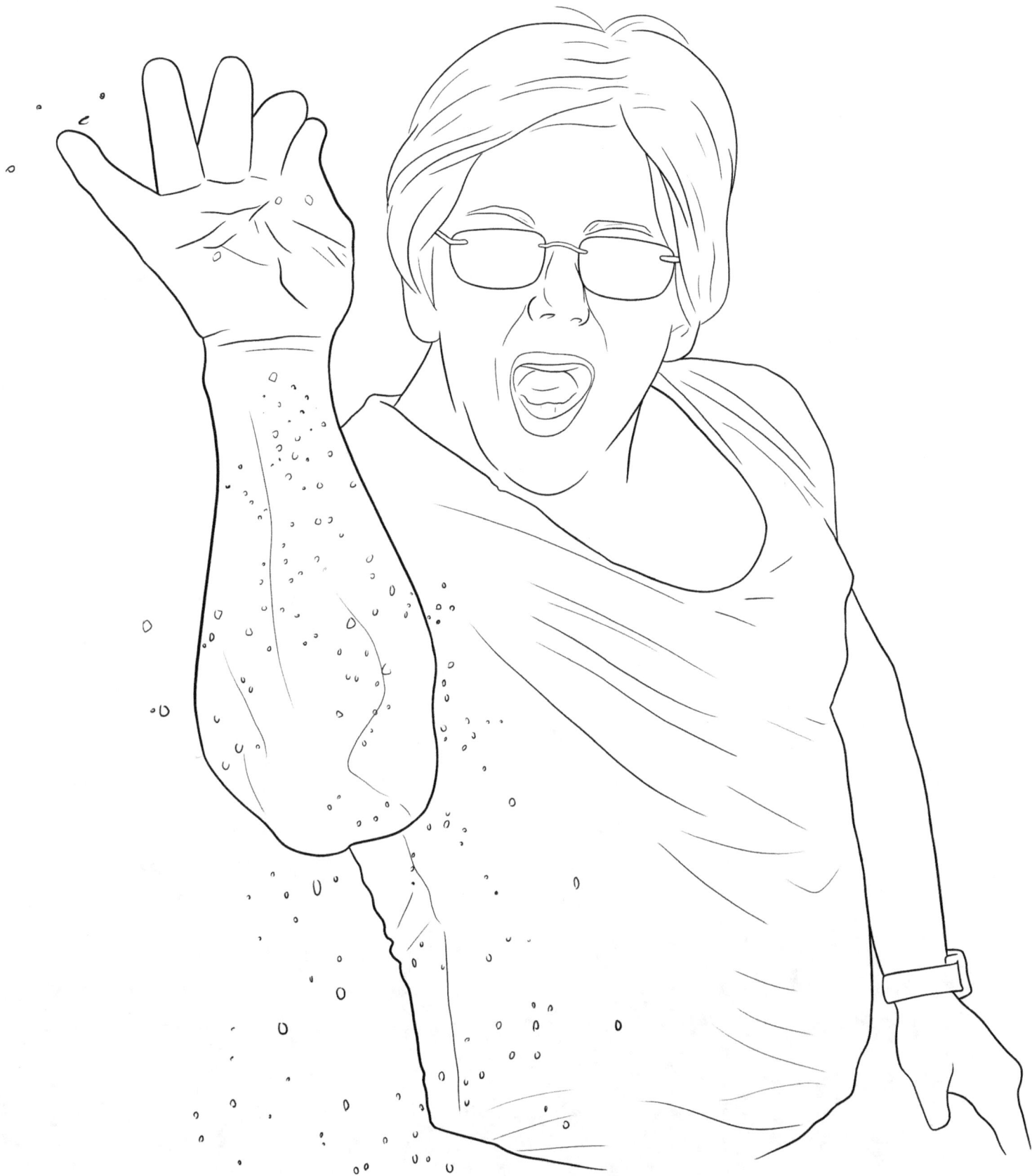

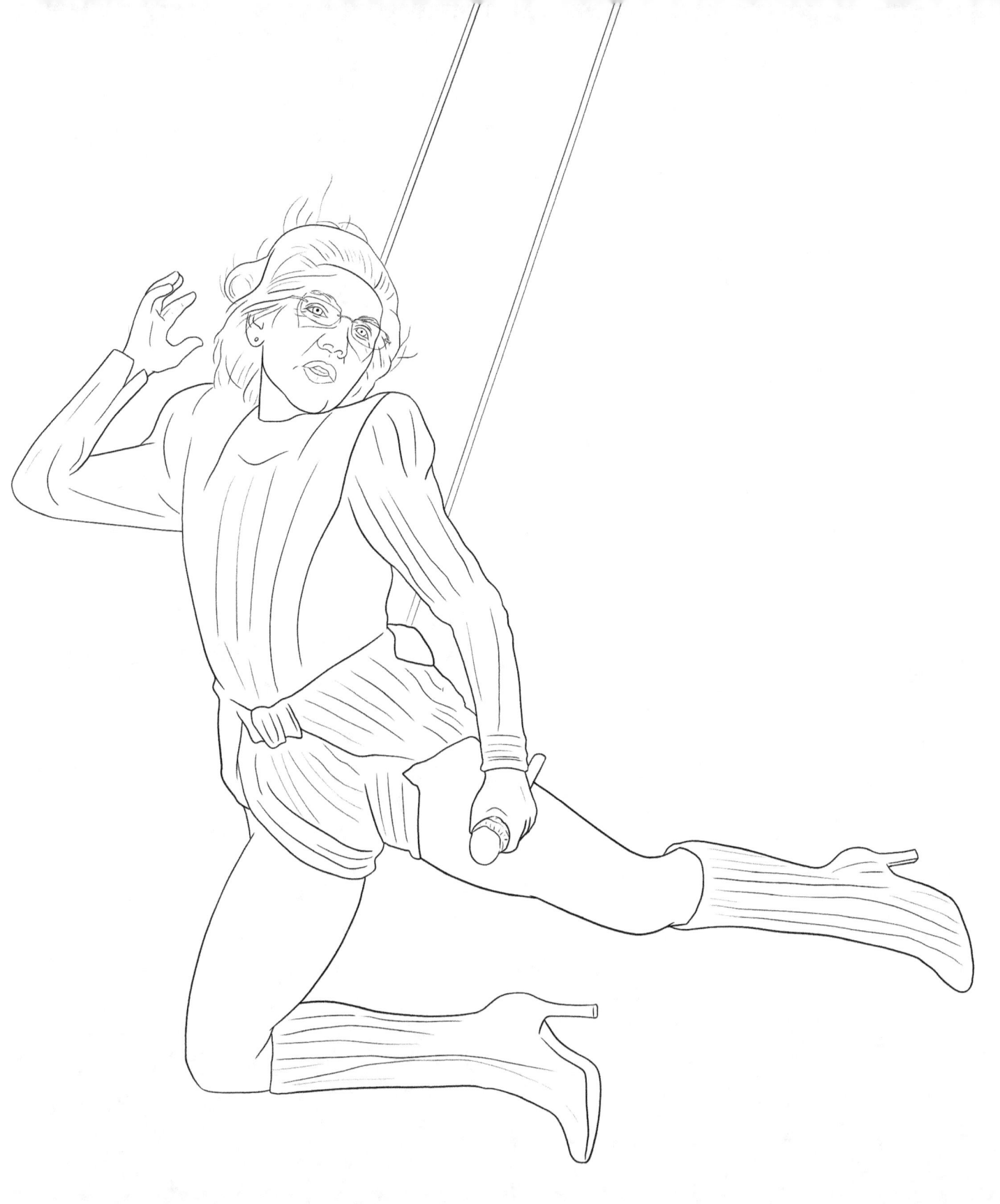

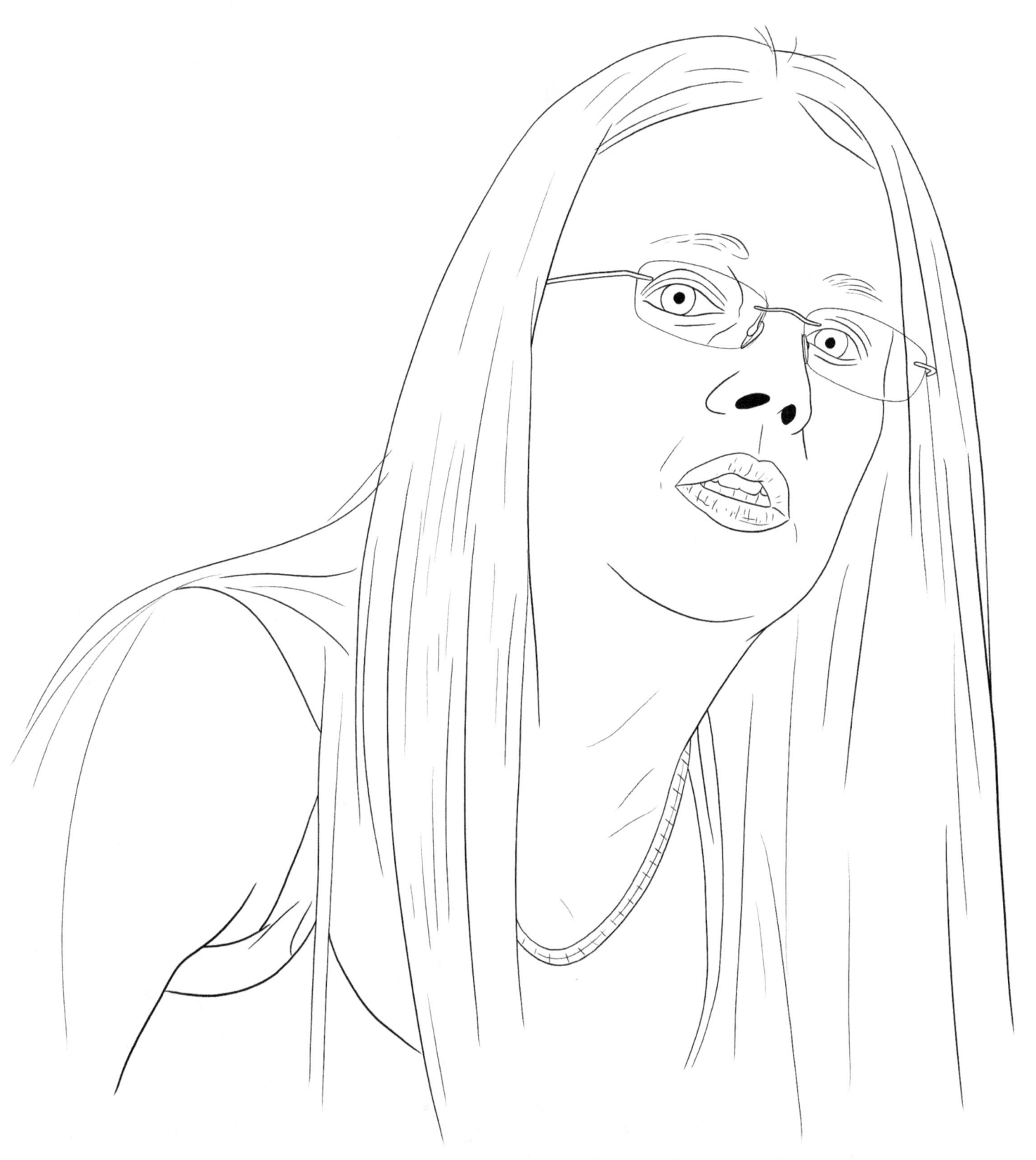

Cash Me Outside
How Bout Dat

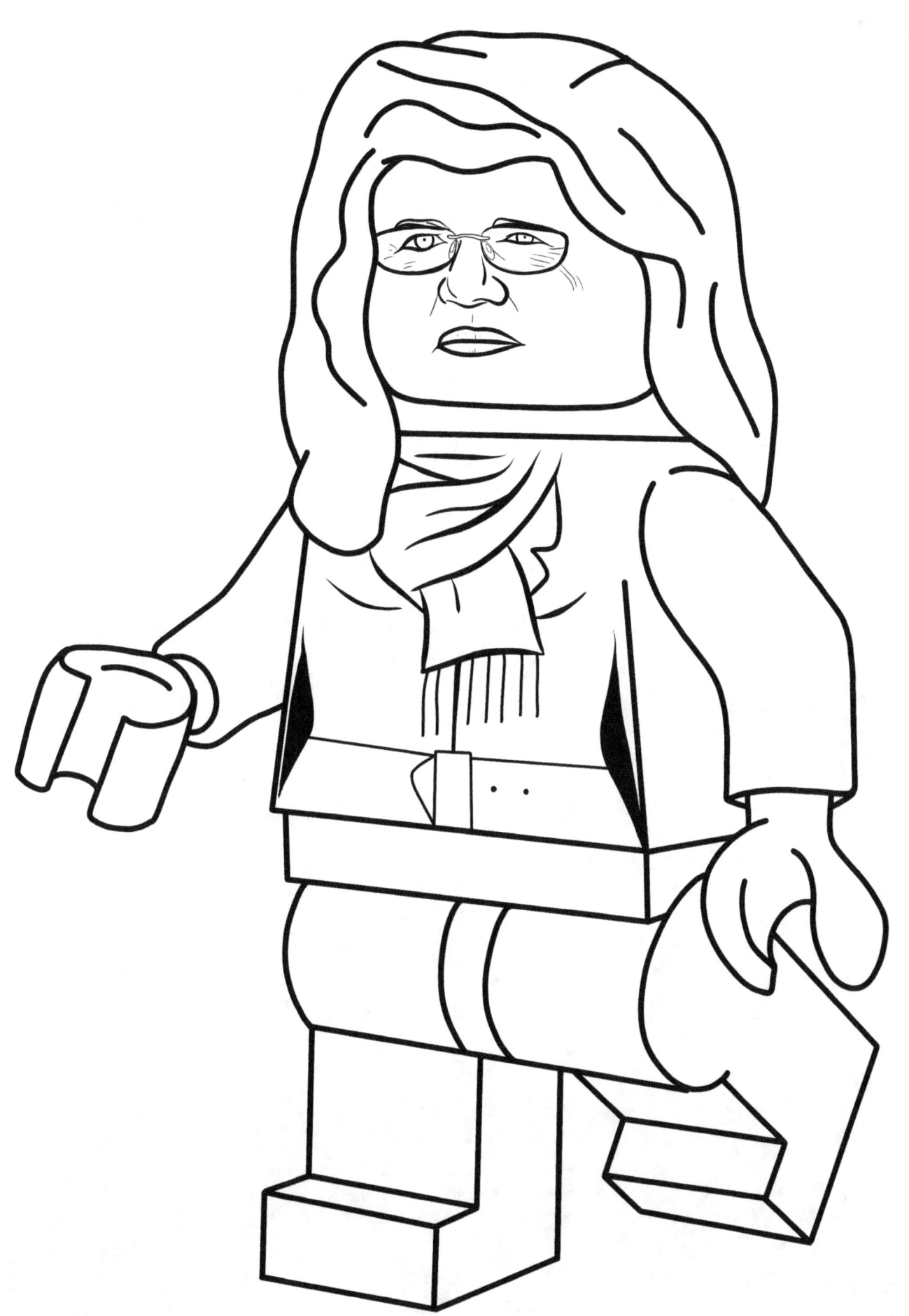

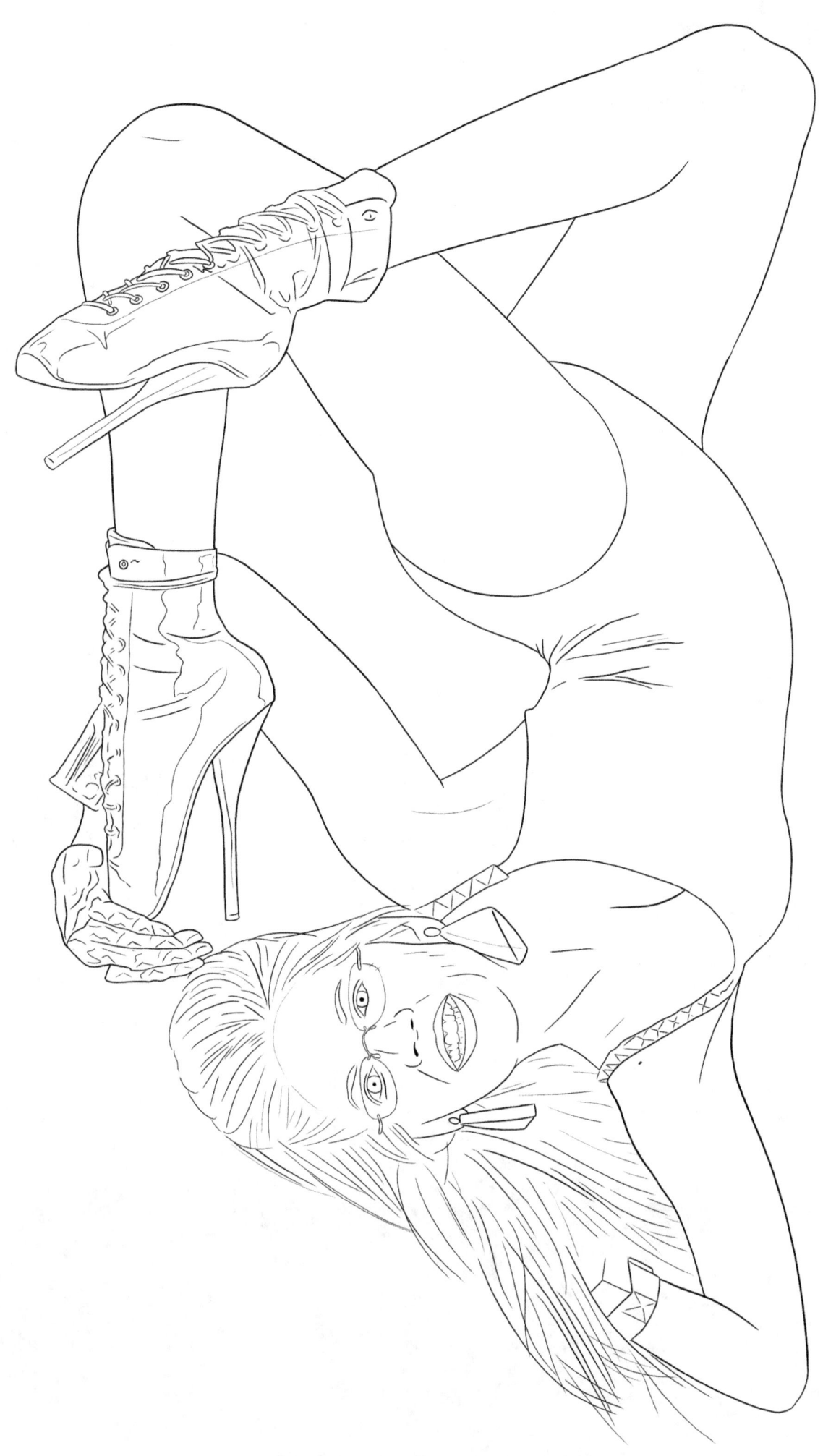

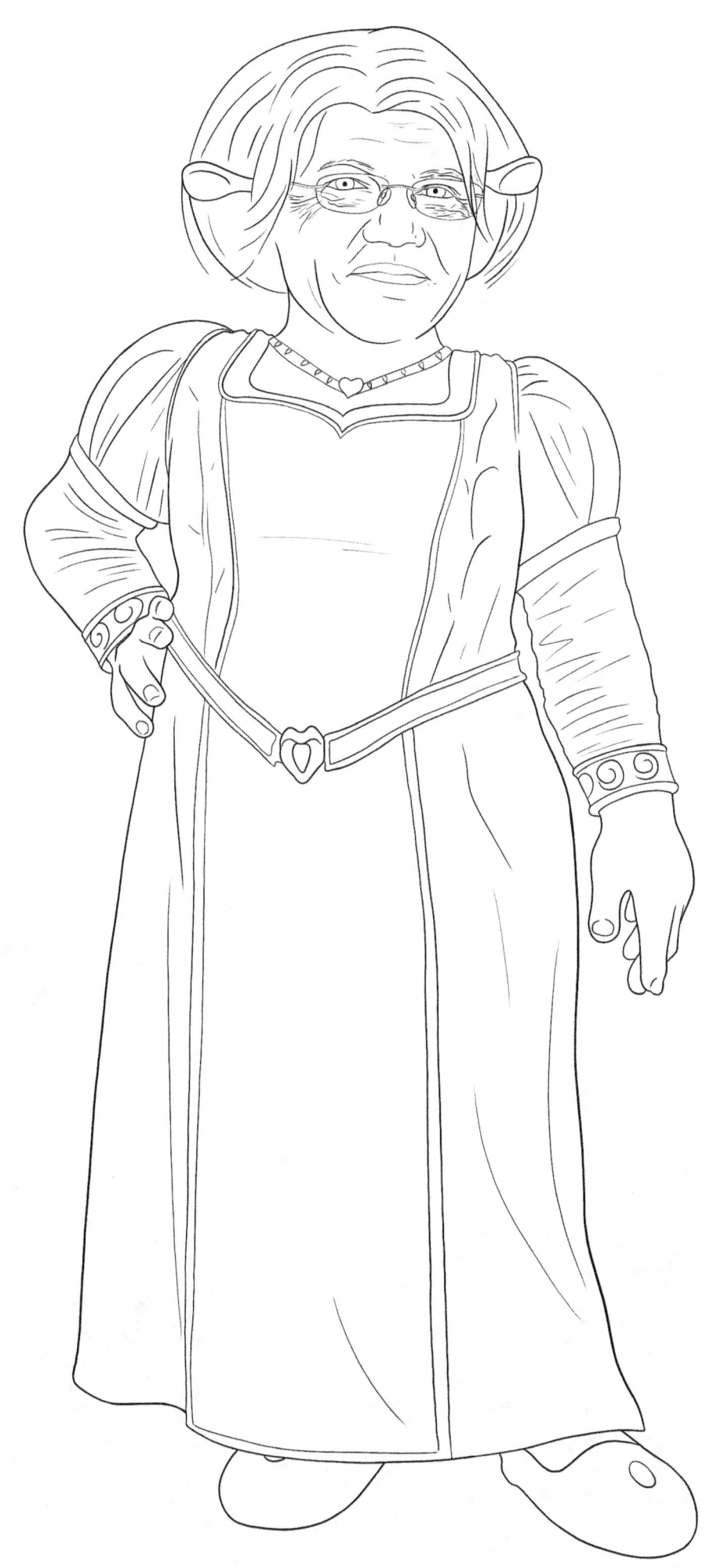

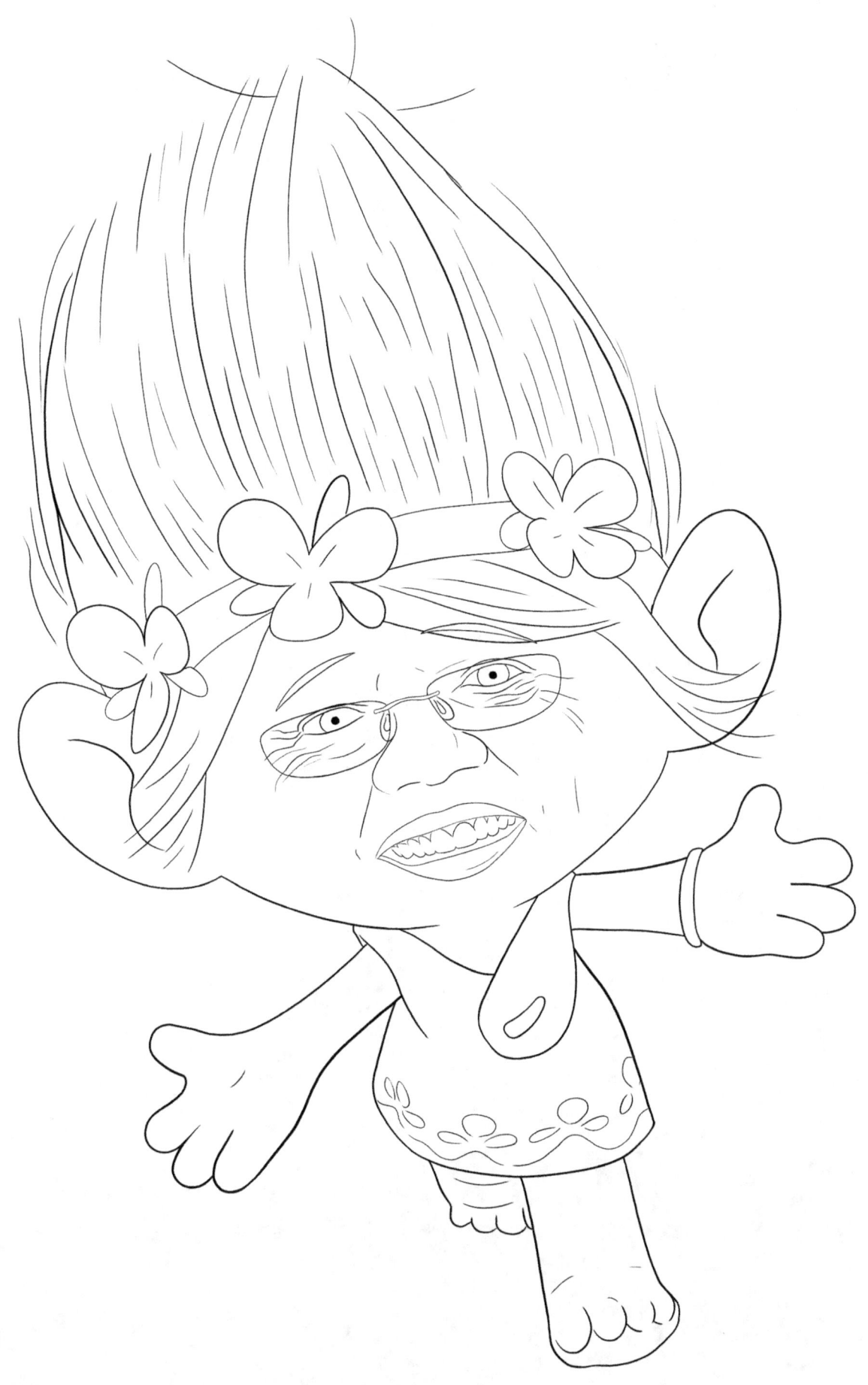

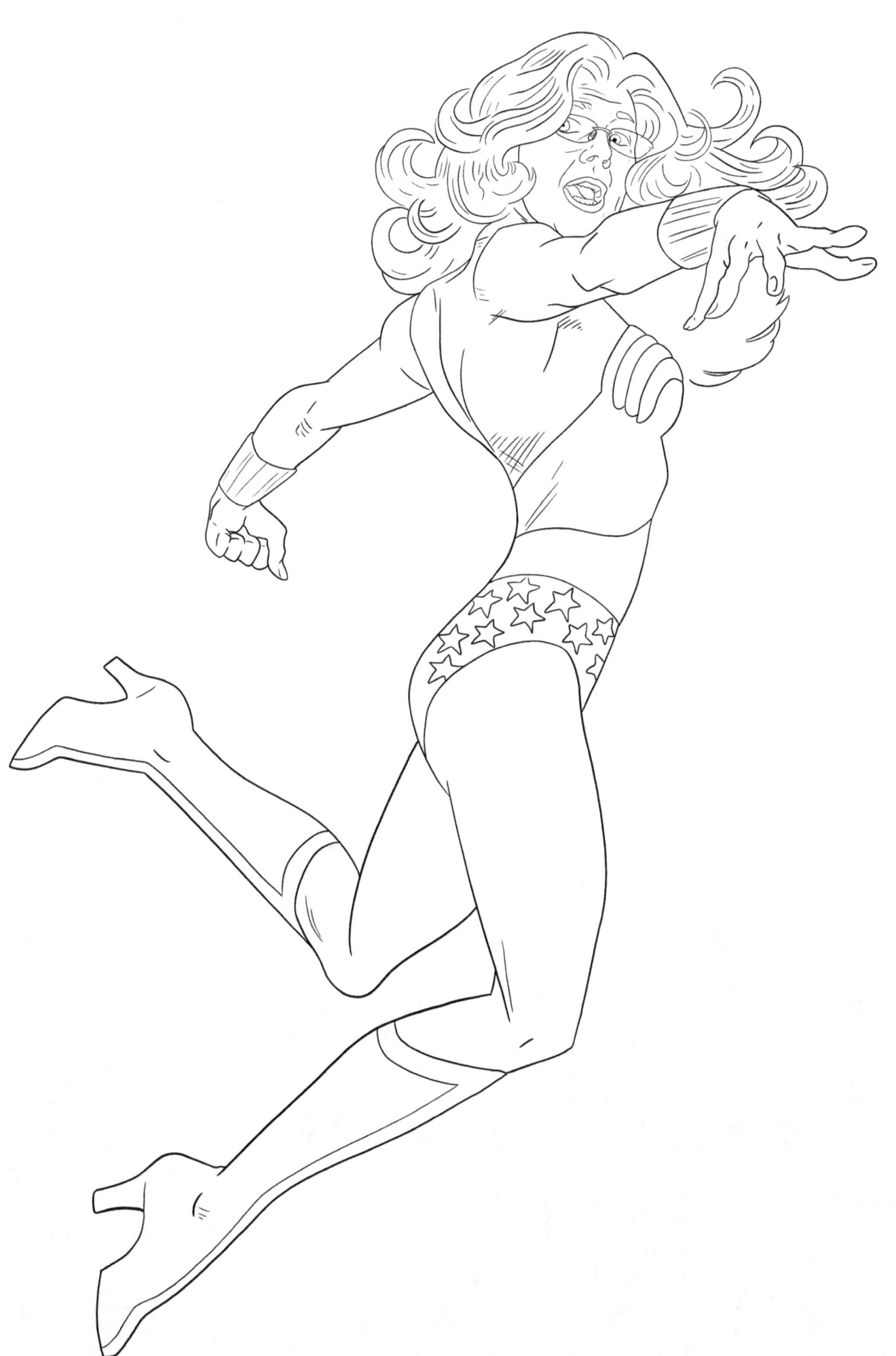

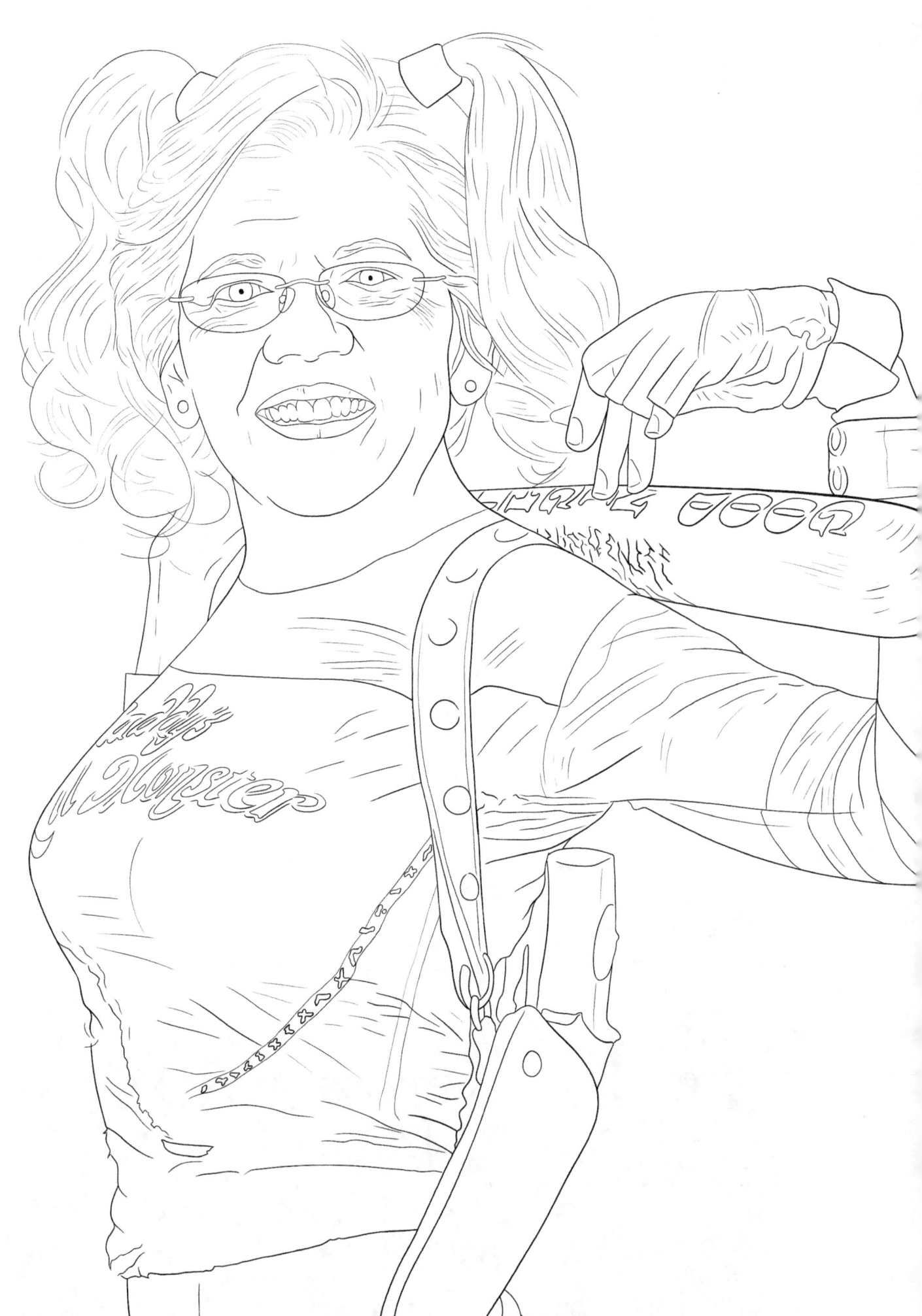

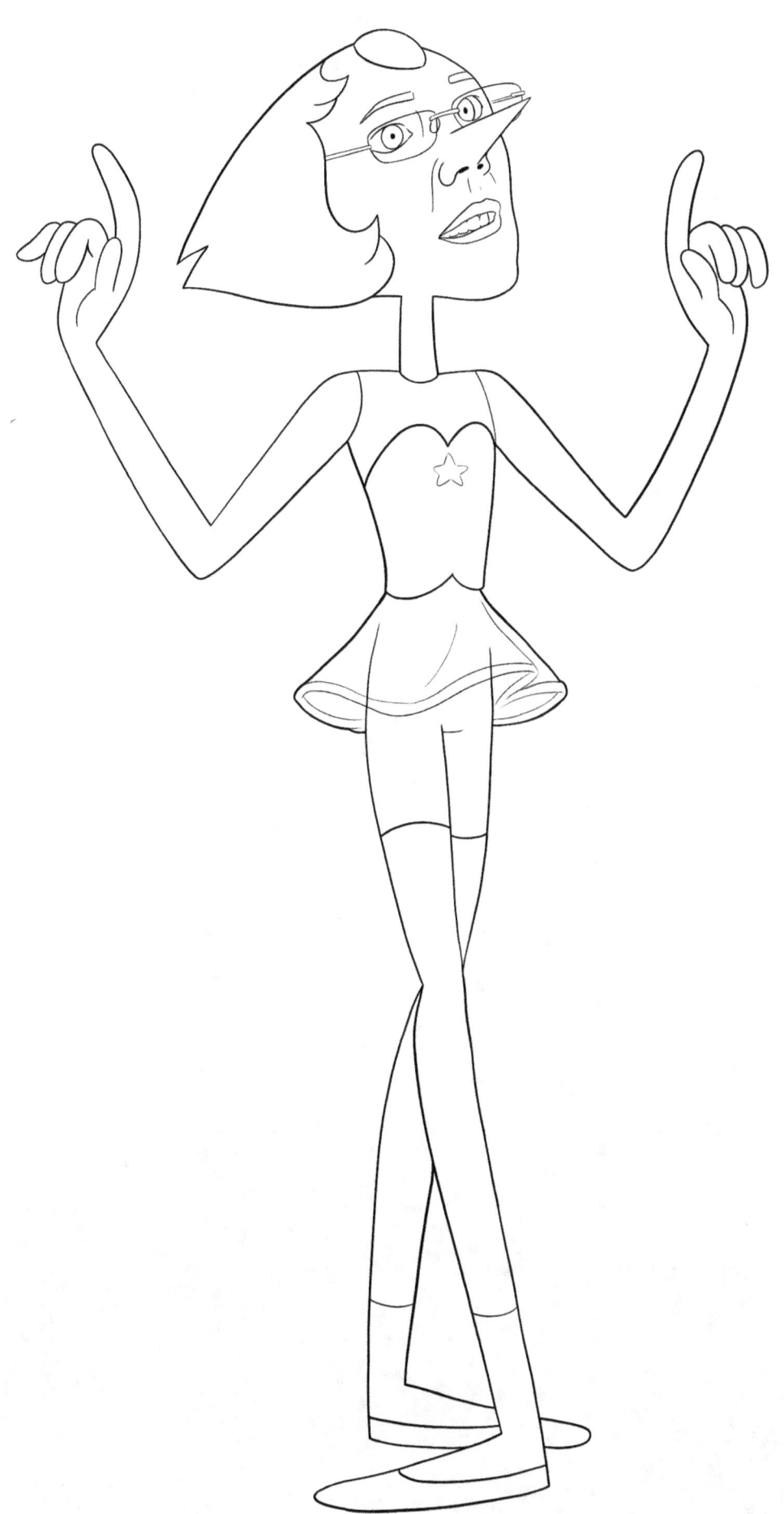

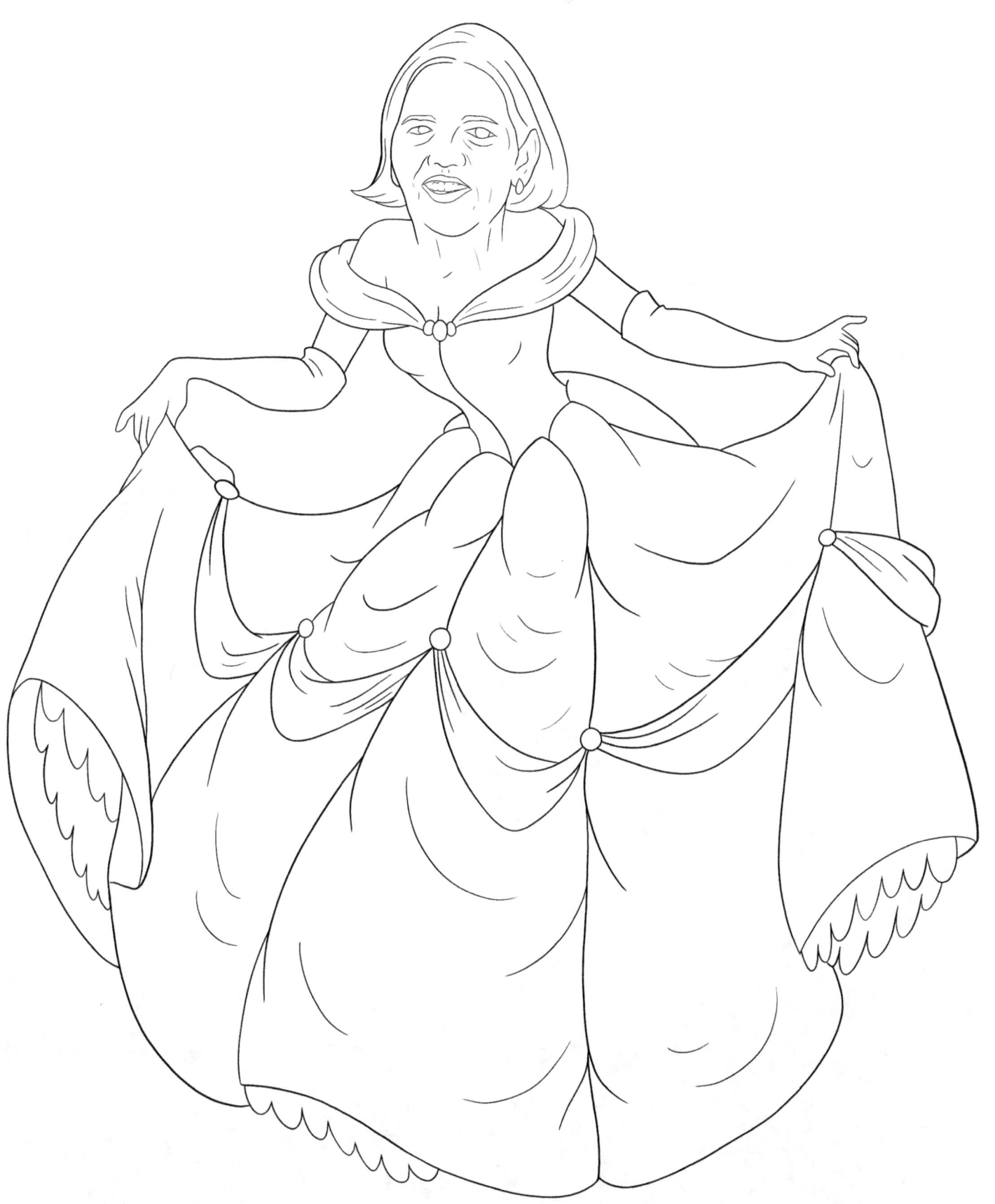

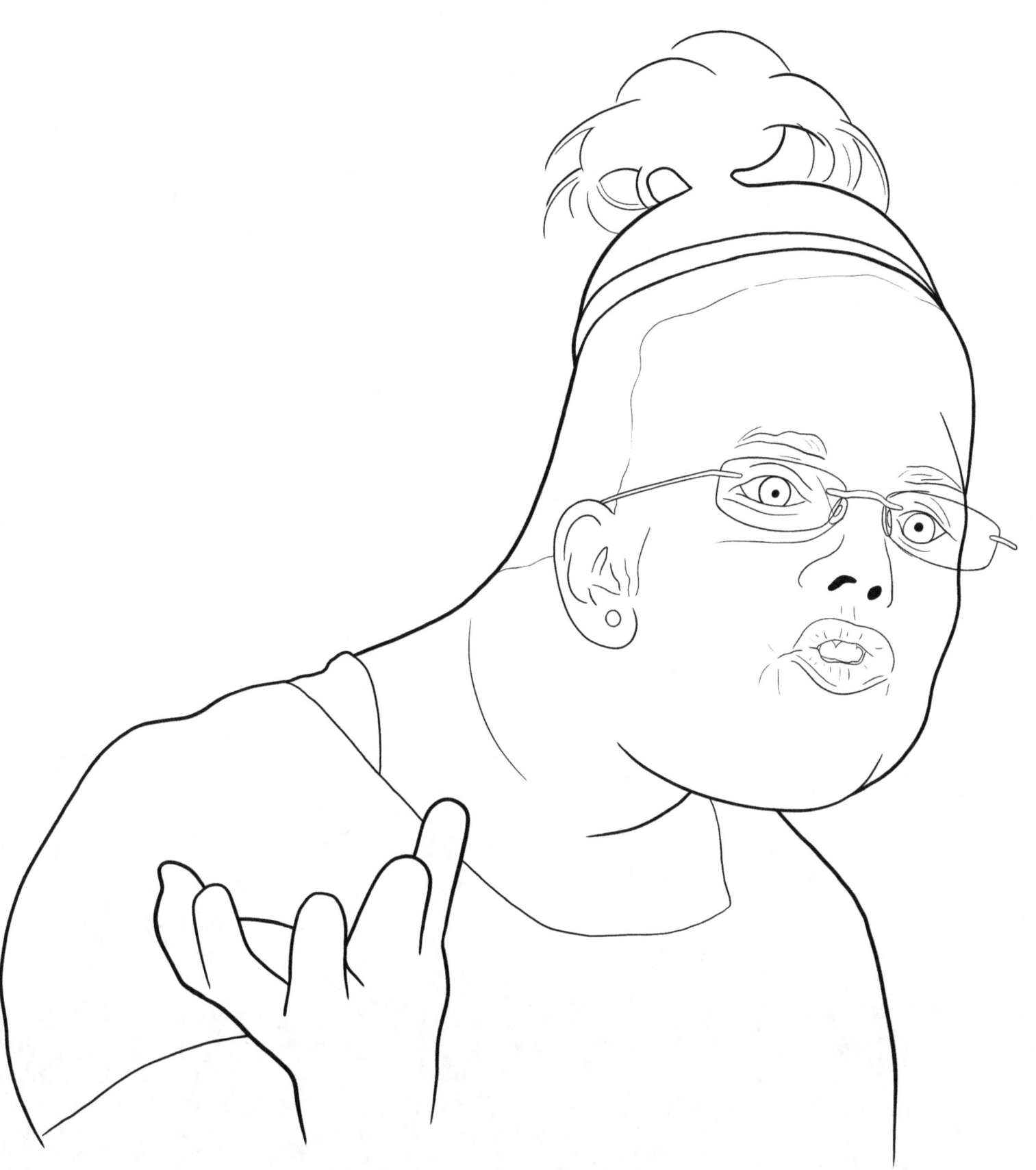

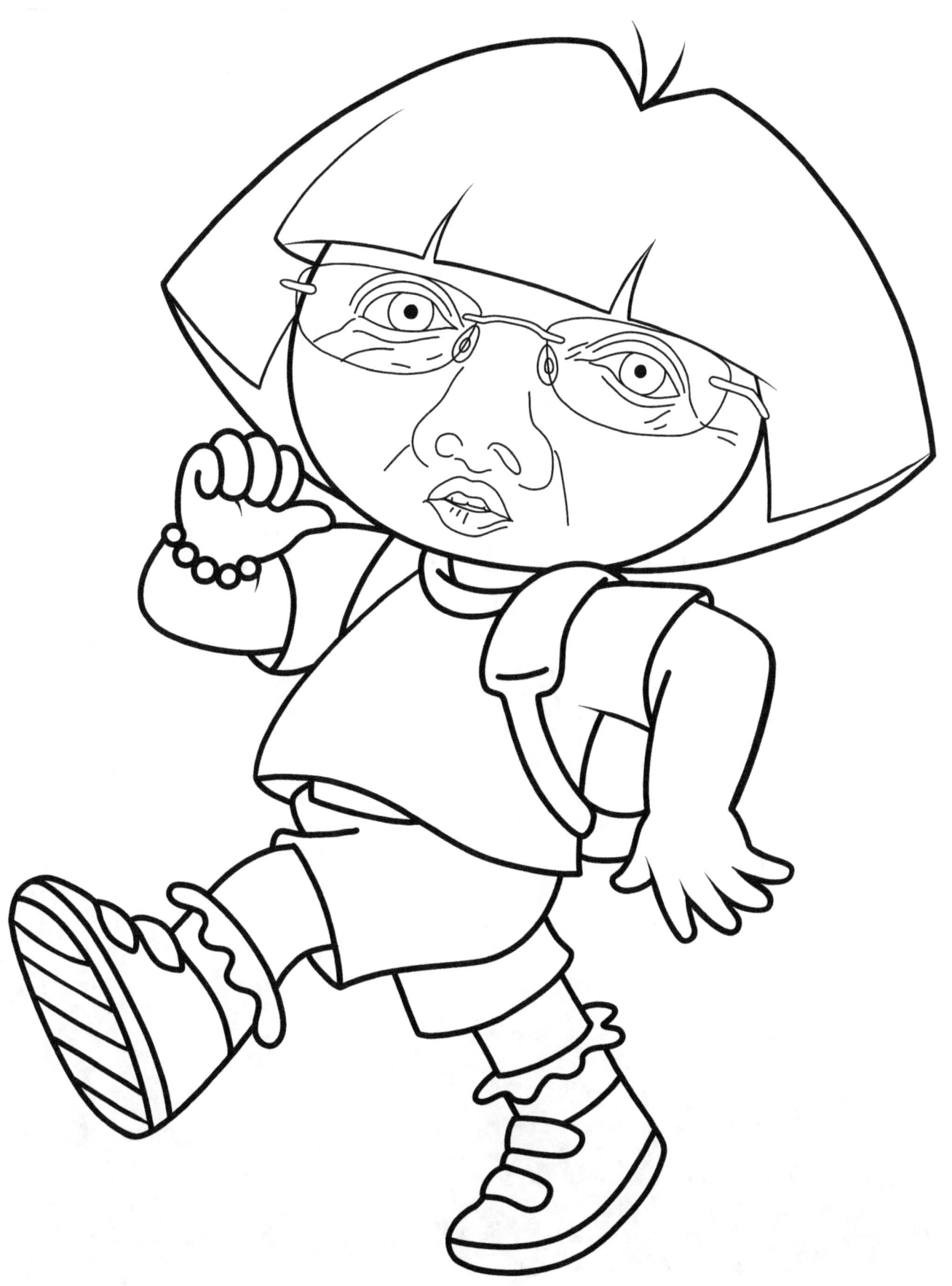

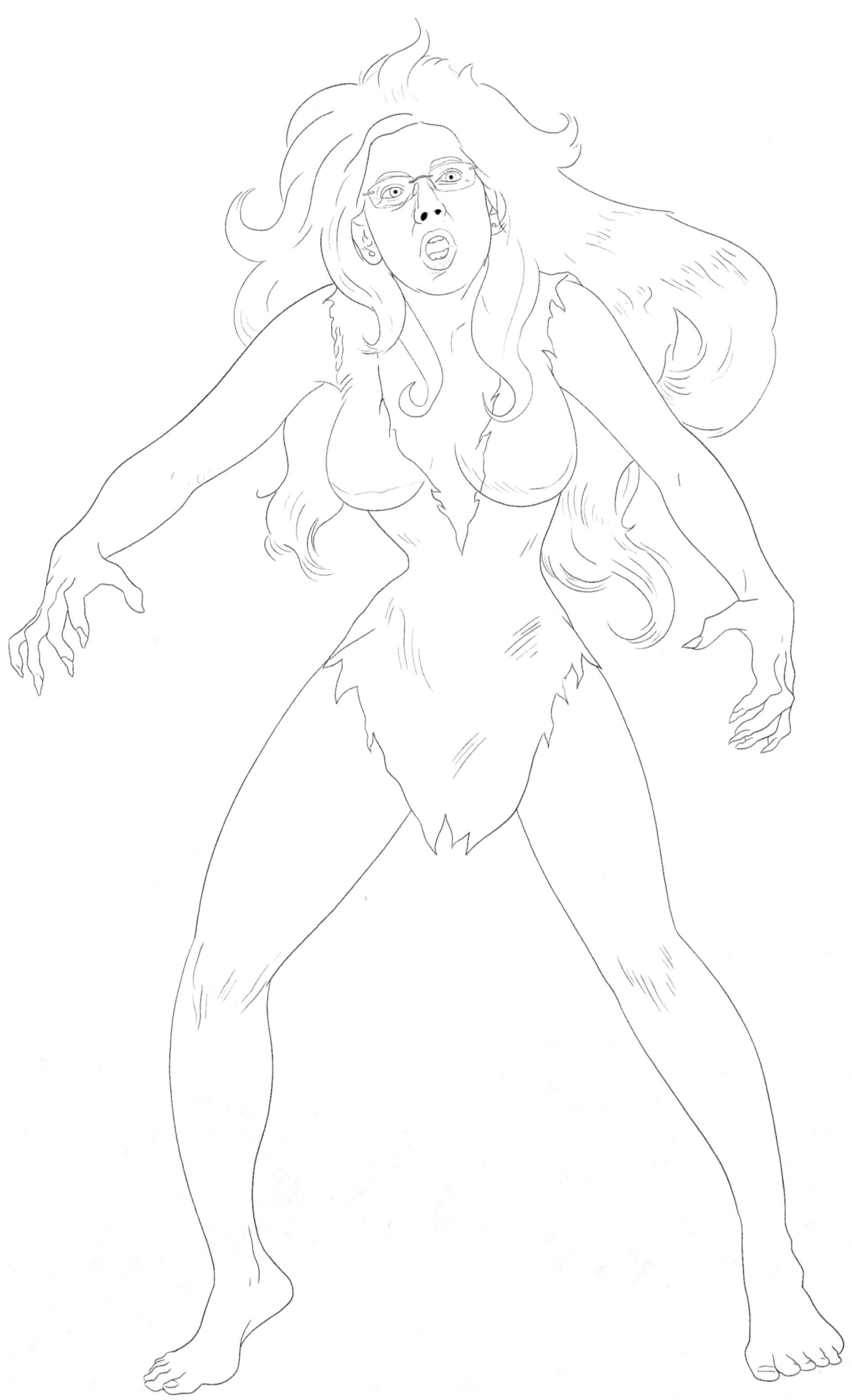

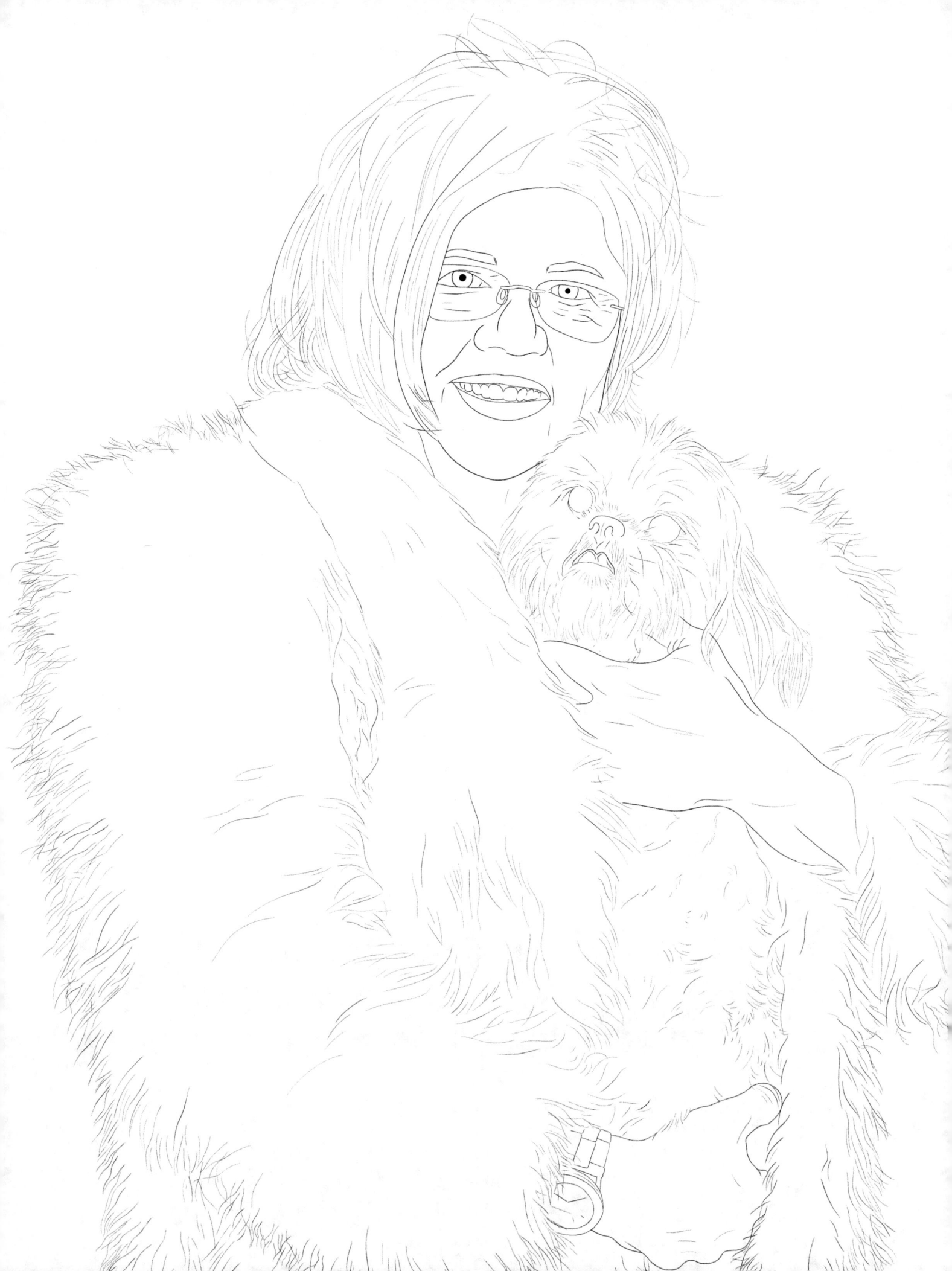

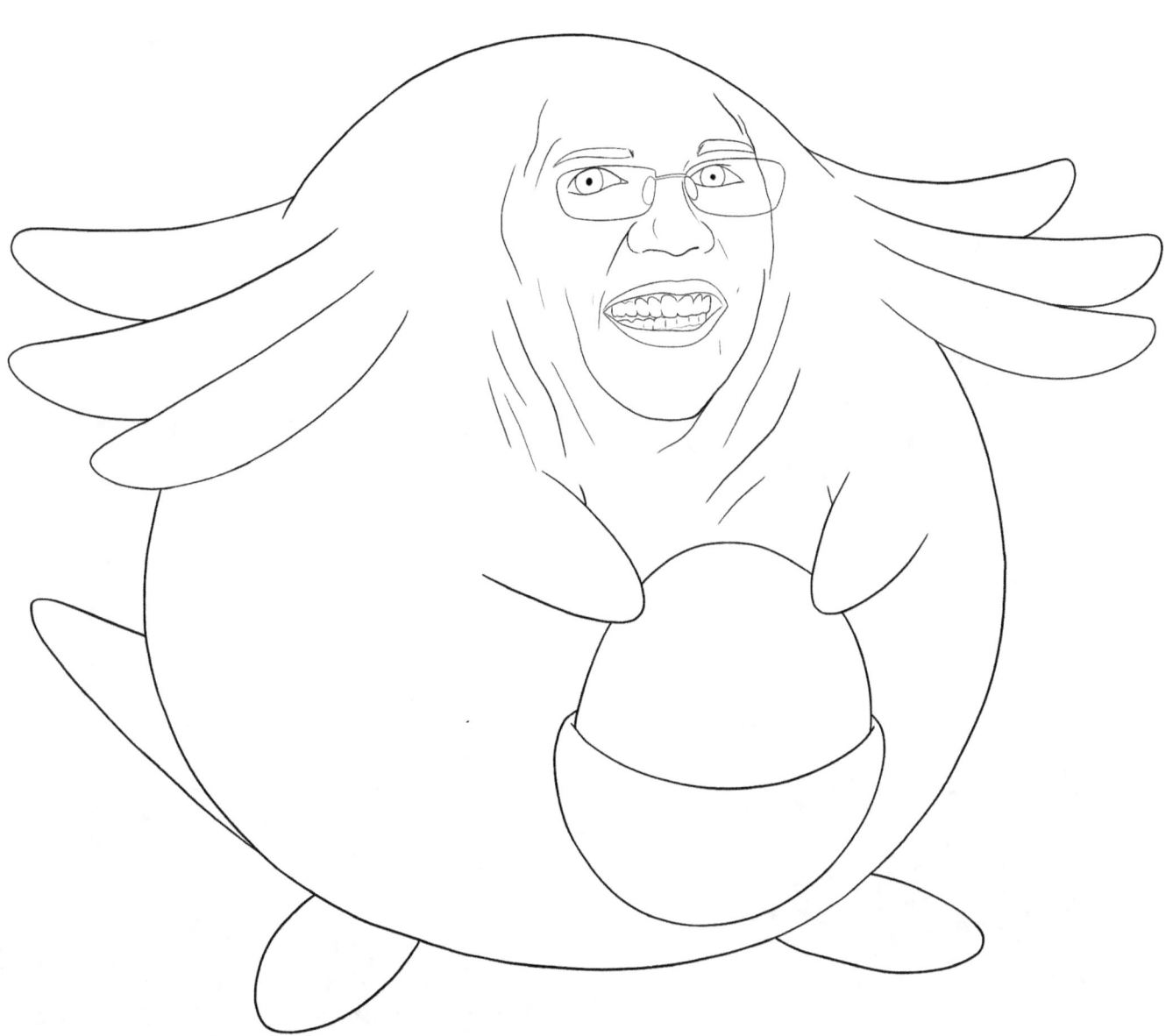

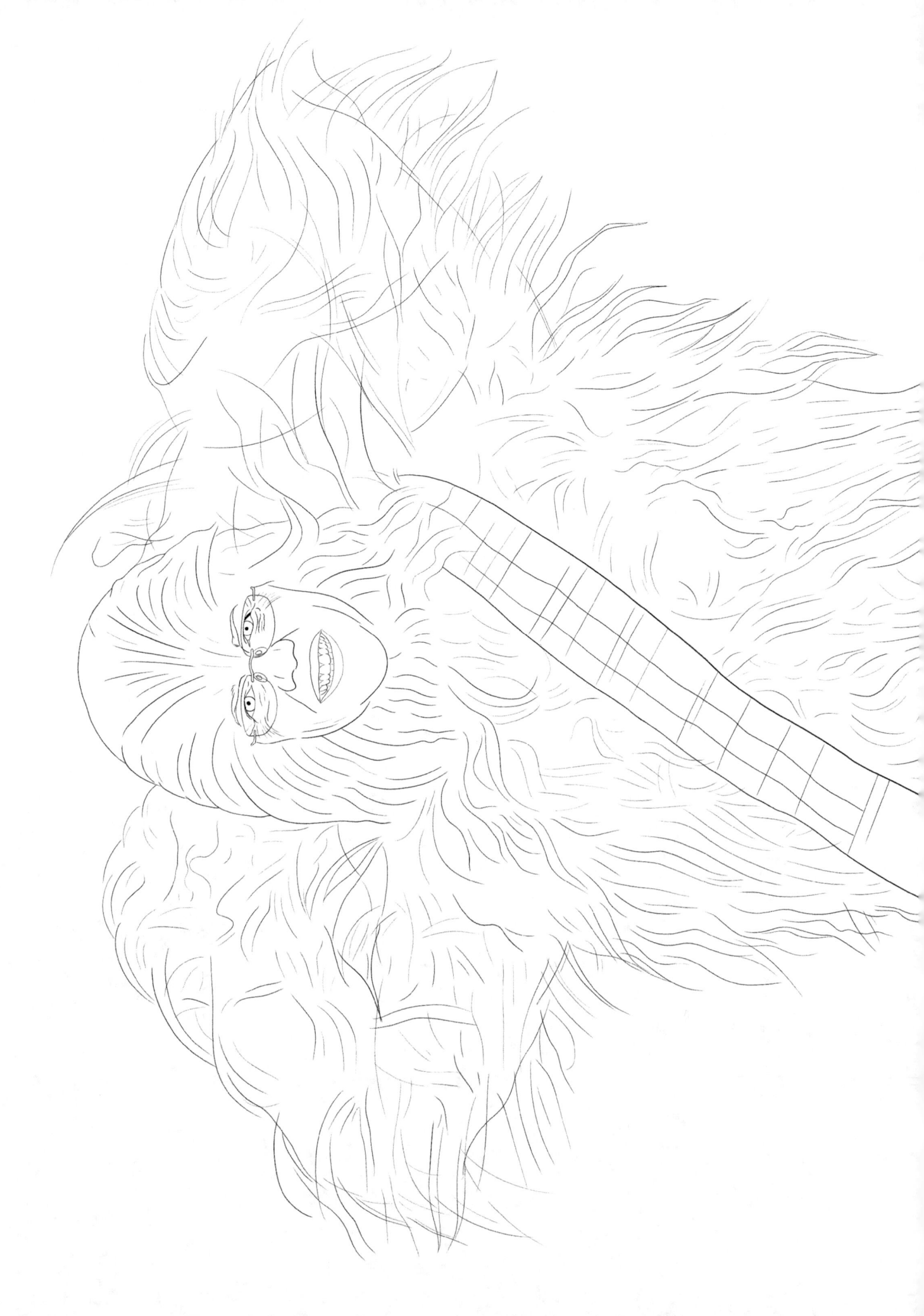

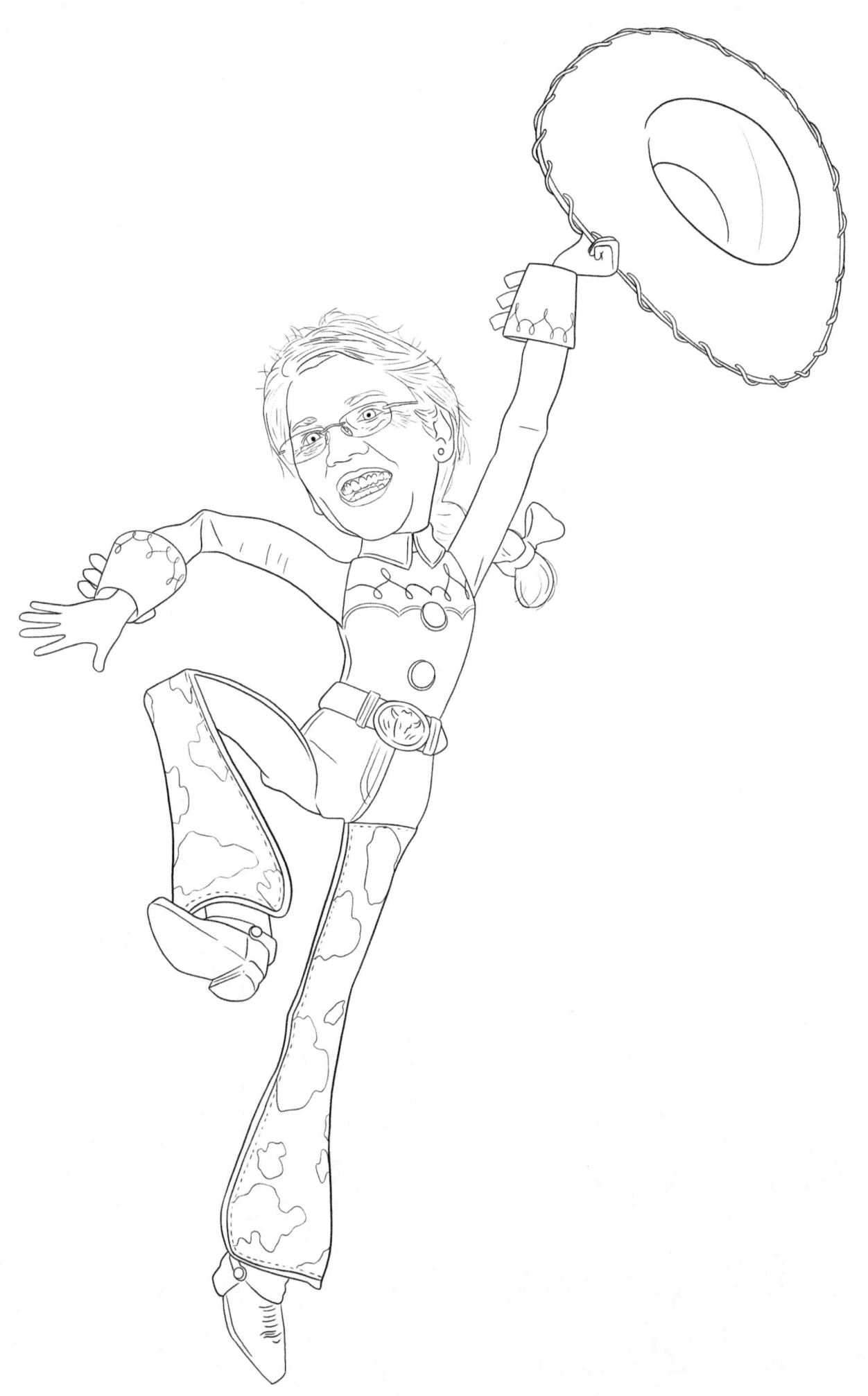

You may also enjoy
Color Me Bernie

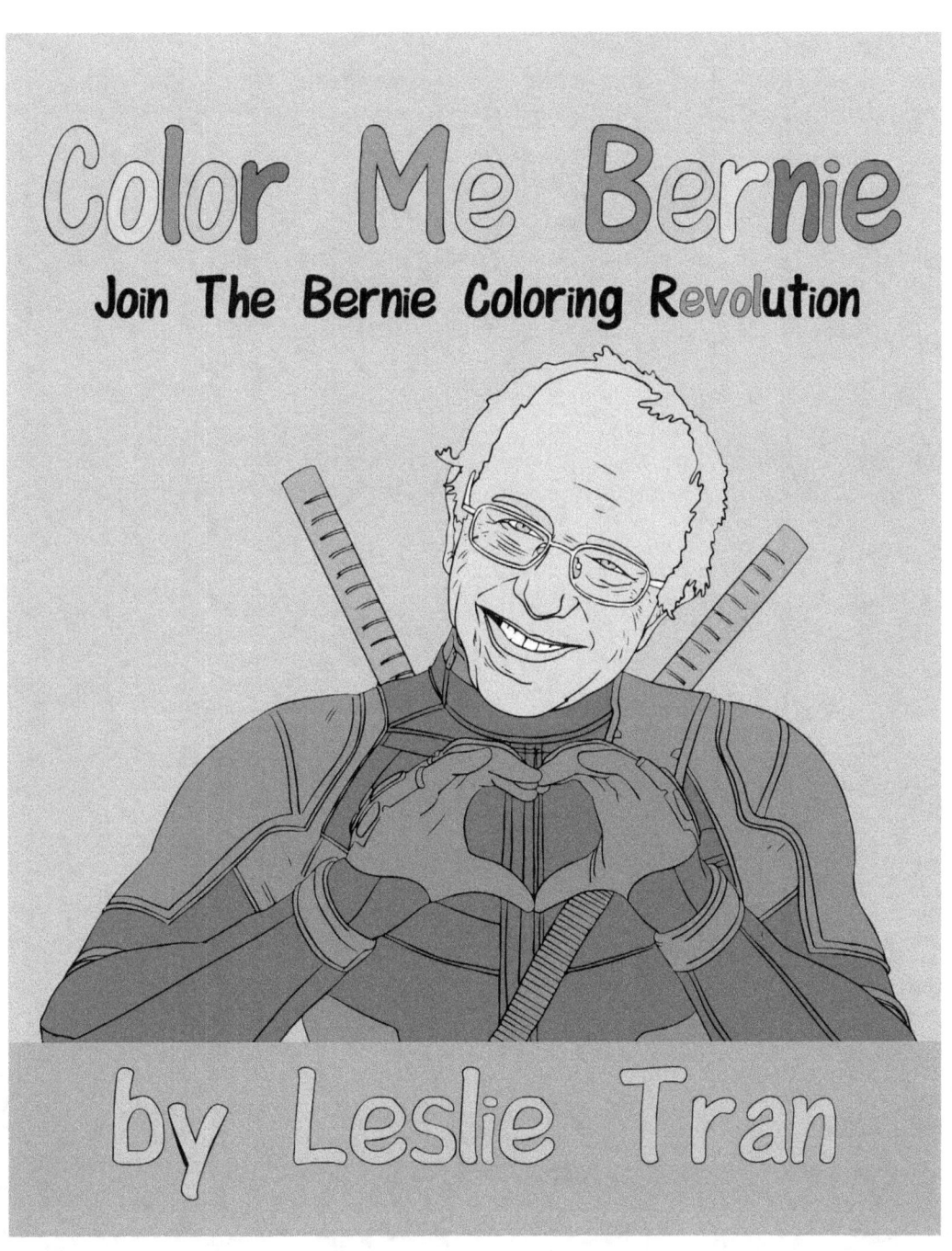